# Teaching American History with the Internet

## Grades K-6

A companion Web site for
this book is maintained at:
http://www.classroom.net/twi/amhistk6

# Teaching American History with the Internet

## Grades K-6
### Internet Lesson Plans and Classroom Activities

*Produced by the Staff of Classroom Connect,*
*creators of premier Internet products for K–12 educators*

**Michael D. Headings,** *Writer*
**Tara Houston,** *Contributing Editor*
**Kathleen Housley,** *Senior Editor*

classroom
**CONNECT**
*Internet made easy in the classroom*™
1866 Colonial Village Lane
Lancaster, Pennsylvania 17601
URL: http://www.classroom.net
Email: connect@classroom.net
( 8 0 0 )   6 3 8 - 1 6 3 9

*Editorial Assistant:* Sam Gorgone
*Design:* John Svatek
*Layout*: Dawn Ranck

ISBN 0-932577-64-4

 Contents

# Lesson Plans: Grades 4-6

# Introduction

A familiar comment often uttered by grade school history students is: "Why do we have to study this?" In the past, students learned about history only through the "eyes" of a single textbook company. Today, the Internet makes history come alive for students, and therefore, more meaningful. Instead of just reading a textbook, the Internet gives students access to primary sources such as diaries, historical documents, and speeches of people who actually lived through and witnessed the events they're studying. This allows students to become the primary filter through which understanding is passed.

The resources in this book, such as diaries and actual historic documents, have been selected because they explain history in a first-person manner. The activities in the book help students understand how these historical accounts are important to the development of the United States and to their lives. Experiencing history through the eyes of people who actually lived brings a whole new level of appreciation to its study.

This book presents students with historical views from a variety of perspectives. We see history through the eyes of early colonists, runaway slaves, and immigrants coming through Ellis Island. By examining the actual words of some of these historic people, students can move beyond memorization into analysis and evaluation of their motives. Students can also look at historical events from multiple perspectives. Students will realize that the study of history is much more than learning a string of facts; it is a quest to understand the perspectives, motivations, and actions of human beings.

The study of history also promotes an understanding of how present day issues are related to and have a historic relationship to events of the past. The lessons in this book have been designed to connect events of our nation's history with the feelings, attitudes, and actions of individuals who lived during a particular time. This personal connection will help students better understand the issues that face them as well. Hopefully, it will also help answer the ever-present question: "Why are we studying this?"

# American History

*Grades K-3*

# A Tour of Plymouth Plantation

## Overview

Students examine actual photographs of the Plimoth [Plymouth] Plantation in Massachusetts, and discover what the homes of the Pilgrims looked like and how they lived their daily lives in those times. The second half of this tour includes sites from Hobbamock's Homesite. This site includes photos of a Native American hamlet.

## Materials

- Computer with Internet access

## Objectives

- View photographs of the Plimoth Plantation and a Native American Hamlet
- Compare and contrast the homes of the Pilgrims to those of the Native American hamlet

## Procedure

**1** Before beginning this lesson, students should have background information about the Pilgrims. They should be able to define or explain the following: Pilgrims and their reasons for coming to the New World; and the hardships that they faced.

**❷** To open this lesson, have the class brainstorm as a group all the things they know about the Pilgrims, then list a dozen things that they'd like to know. Tell the students they will be investigating what it was like to be a Pilgrim boy or girl, and to discover what it was like to be a Native American in that time period.

**❸** Have students begin their investigation by going to this Web site:

**A Walking Tour of Plimoth Plantation**
URL: http://spirit.lib.uconn.edu/ArchNet/Topical/Historic/
    Plimoth/Plimoth.html

This will connect students to a page describing the Plantation project and provide your students with a list of connecting links to view homes or some aspect of the two cultures. Students simply need to scroll down and click on the highlighted link to be taken to a page with the photograph and description. [With beginning readers, you may want to escort small groups on the tour. This is also an excellent activity for your class to conduct with their reading buddies in an upper grade.]

**❹** Have the students compare and contrast the homes of the Pilgrims to those of the Native American Hamlet using a Venn diagram on the accompanying worksheet. Once students have completed this activity, have them share their projects with the rest of the class.

**❺** Have the students review their earlier listing of everything they knew about Pilgrims. Were there any misconceptions? What new things did they discover. As a culminating event, have the class as a whole complete a big Venn diagram showing the similarities and the differences between how the Pilgrims and Native American's lived. On a big poster, draw a Venn diagram and have students contribute additions to the diagram. Post on the bulletin board and add the children's projects to the display.

# Extensions

**1** Students can gain information about another U.S. colonial town called Jamestown. Students can read about the history of Jamestown by opening the following connection:

**Jamestown Rediscovery**
URL: http://www.widomaker.com/~apva/history/index.html

**2** Students can then view photos of the Jamestown exhibit by opening the following site:

**Jamestown Exhibit**
URL: http://www.widomaker.com/~apva/exhibit/index.html

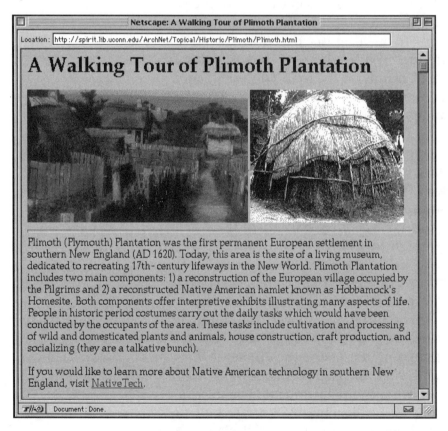

**A Walking Tour of Plimoth Plantation**
URL: http://spirit.lib.uconn.edu/ArchNet/Topical/Historic/Plimoth/Plimoth.html

# A Tour of Plymouth Plantation

Student name: _____

Date: _____

Compare and contrast the homes of the Pilgrims to those of Native Americans

Pilgrims

Native Americans

# Draw a Picture

Draw a picture of a home of a Pilgrim and a home of a Native American. How are they different? How are they similar?

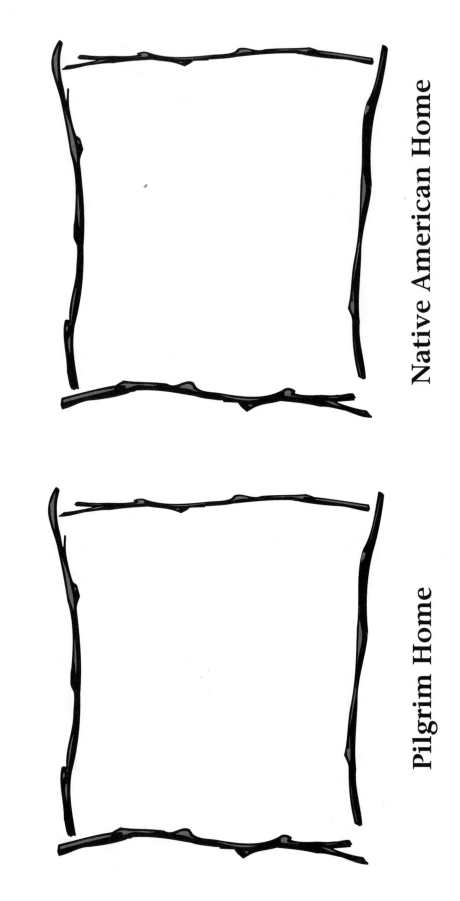

**Native American Home**

**Pilgrim Home**

**Activity Sheet**   A Tour of Plymouth Plantation

# A Virtual Tour of Philadelphia

## Overview

Students will tour parts of historic Philadelphia. Students will be able to view such sites as the Liberty Bell, Independence Hall, and the United States Mint from their computer.

## Materials

- Computer with Internet access

## Objectives

- Identify historic sites of Philadelphia
- Identify two facts about each site

## Procedure

1 To prepare students for this lesson establish some background information for students. It is important for students to understand that one of the major cities in colonial America was Philadelphia. Explain to your students that at this point in history the United States was struggling to become independent from England. Tell them that this struggle for independence was centered in the Philadelphia area. This was the site where Thomas

Jefferson wrote the Declaration of Independence and where it was signed. Philadelphia was also the center for many other important historical figures such as Benjamin Franklin who invented many things and started the first post office and fire department.

❷ Tell students that they will be taking a virtual tour of the city of Philadelphia. Have them open the following Internet site:

**Historic Philadelphia**
URL: http://www.libertynet.org/iha/virtual.html

At this site the students can go through a preprogrammed virtual tour by simply scrolling down and clicking on the arrow that says "next stop." However, using this method creates the problem of having students view every site in the tour whether those sites are relevant to your lesson or not. A recommended option is to have the students scroll down the screen until they find each site listed separately. At this point on the page, students can simply click on that site. That way you can be selective about which sites you'd like them to visit on their tour. The following are worth viewing: Liberty Bell, Independence Hall, Gaff House, Franklin Court, Betsy Ross House, United States Mint, and Christ Church.

**Teacher's note:** Some of these sites include sound clips and all the sites include not only pictures, but excellent descriptions of the site. Have the students read these descriptions.

❸ After the students have completed their tour, have students draw a representation of their favorite site on the tour using the facts collected from their virtual visit. Students must include a brief description of the site, to convince others that this historic site should be on everyone's trip agenda if they visit Philadelphia. Have students share their drawings with the rest of the class.

**8**

**Lesson Plan** A Virtual Tour of Philadelphia
...................................................................................
Teaching American History with the Internet

# Extensions

**1** Students may simply enjoy viewing the other virtual tour sites that you did not use in the classroom tour. Give students the opportunity to explore the other sites listed in the index.

**2** Have students research historic people of Philadelphia such as Ben Franklin. Students can gain information about this historic figure by connecting to the following Internet site:

**Ben Franklin**
URL: http://www.windows.umich.edu/people/
enlightenment/franklin.html

**Historic Philadelphia**
URL: http://www.libertynet.org/iha/virtual.html

# Benjamin Franklin: Inventor

## Overview

Benjamin Franklin is one of America's most famous historic figures. He was known as an inventor, statesman, scientist, and author. This lesson will help students better understand Franklin as an American inventor.

## Materials

- Computer with Internet access
- White construction paper

## Objectives

- View inventions of Benjamin Franklin
- Design an invention
- Use an online connect-the-dot activity to view a Franklin stove

## Procedure

**1** Ask students to brainstorm why they think people invent new things. Lead them to understand that there is a need and someone tries to fulfill that need.

**2** Then have students brainstorm things in their home that make life easier for them. Examples: dishwasher, washer/dryer, stove, etc.

**3** Tell students that they will be viewing some inventions by Benjamin Franklin.

**Benjamin Franklin: Inventor**
URL: http://sln.fi.edu/franklin/inventor/inventor.html

**4** With emergent readers, the teacher can read the background information on each invention, or beginners can work in pairs to read the content. To view the invention, simply click on the link that is in the text and in blue lettering.

**5** Have students try to determine why Benjamin Franklin wanted to invent those items.

**6** Then have students take a blank piece of paper and design an invention that would help them with some activity or make their life easier. For example: a machine that makes their bed or a machine to complete homework.

**7** Have students share their ideas with each other.

**8** As a final activity, have students connect to the following site:

**Benjamin Franklin - Stove**
URL: http://www.energy.ca.gov/energy/education/ben/
    ben-html/stove3.html

This site is an online connect-the-dot page. Students can connect the dots to reveal another of Franklin's inventions: the Franklin stove. [If time is an element, you can download the page and copy it for the students.]

# Extensions

**1** Have students explore the works of Benjamin Franklin the scientist. Students can view some of his experiments at the following site:

**Benjamin Franklin: Scientist**
URL: http://sln.fi.edu/franklin/scientst/scientst.html

Then have students perform a simple experiment on electricity which can be found at the following site:

**Shooting Puffed Rice**
URL: gopher://ec.sdcs.k12.ca.us:70/00/lessons/
ucsd_InterNet_Lessons/Physical_Science_and_Chemistry/
Electricity/Shooting_Puffed_Rice.txt

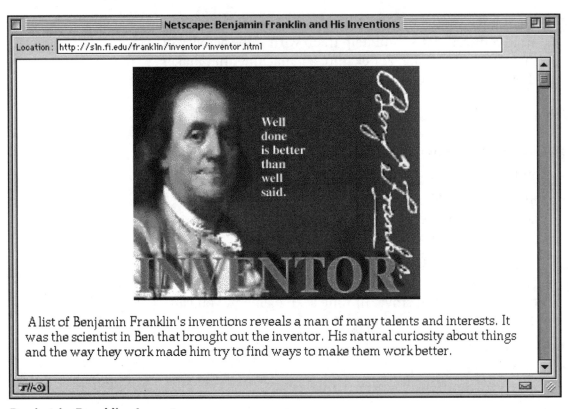

**Benjamin Franklin: Inventor**
URL: http://sln.fi.edu/franklin/inventor/inventor.html

# The American Flag

## Overview

The American flag has evolved as the United States developed over the years. In this lesson, the students will see the flag's evolution and will reflect on the reasons for the changes. They will also develop an understanding that symbols are important to nations.

## Materials

- Computer with Internet access

Objectives

- Compare and contrast the various versions of the American flag
- Discuss the importance of having symbols

Procedure

**1** Write the word "symbol" on the blackboard. Have the students repeat the word. Ask if any student knows what the word "symbol" means or if they can give an example of a symbol. Eventually, try to develop a working definition which makes sense to the students. For example, "a symbol is something which makes you think of an important idea."

**❷** Ask the students if they see any symbols in the classroom. Eventually, guide them to see the American flag. Ask them, "What does the flag stand for?" Accept almost any answer since symbols can have different meanings for different people.

**❸** Ask the students if they think the flag always looked this way. Tell them that they are going to look at some "old" flags on the Internet. Give the students the accompanying worksheet to use as a guide while looking at the various flags at the following Internet site:

**Flag Picture Gallery**
URL: http://libertynet.org/iha/betsy/flagpics.html

Let the students look at the various flags on this site and compare and contrast them using the worksheet.

**❹** Ask the students, "When you see the American flag, what do you think of?" Write these words on the board. Then ask them why they think it is important to have a symbol like the American flag. Ask them if they can think of any other symbols of our country. Have them write down some reasons why it is good to have symbols for our country.

**Flag Picture Gallery**
URL: http://libertynet.org/iha/betsy/flagpics.html

**Lesson Plan**   The American Flag

Teaching American History with the Internet

 # Extensions

**1** Have the students design a flag for their own classroom. First have them brainstorm the important values represented in their classroom (learning is important, respecting others, etc . . . ). Then have them design a flag which will help remind them and others of those important values.

**2** Have your students write a cinquain poem about the flag. A cinquain has five lines:
Line 1: Flag

Line 2: 2 adjectives describing the flag

Line 3: 3 action words related to flags

Line 4: a 4-word phrase about flags

Line 5: a synonym for flag

Every student can do one, but do one as a class as well and publish it online at the following Internet site:

**CyberThoughts about Betsy and the Flag**
URL: http://libertynet.org/iha/betsy/flagmail.html

# The American Flag

**Student name:** _____    **Date:** _____

**Directions:** Find similarities and differences between the flags on the following Internet site:

> **Flag Picture Gallery**
> URL: http://libertynet.org/iha/betsy/flagpics.html

1. How many flags are on this page?

_____

2. How many flags have stripes? How many don't have stripes?

_____

3. What do you think the stripes stand for?

_____

_____

4. Why do you think some flags have stars and some don't?

_____

_____

**Activity Sheet**   The American Flag

5. What do you think the stars stand for?

_____

_____

_____

_____

6. How many stars are on the 1846 flag? Why?

_____

_____

_____

_____

7. How many stars are on the the last 3 flags? Why does the number of stars keep getting larger?

_____

_____

8. Do you think there will ever be another flag with more stars on it? Why or why not?

_____

_____

# Pictures of a Plantation

## Overview

George Washington, our first president, is one of America's most historic figures. Through photographs of George Washington's Mount Vernon Plantation students will be able to gain some insight into the layout of a plantation and the differences in life from that period to current times.

## Materials

- Computer with Internet access
- Large white bulletin board paper
- Plain white paper

 ## Objectives

- Tour the grounds of Mount Vernon
- Draw a layout of a plantation
- Discuss differences between colonial life and modern day life

## Procedure

**1** Have students brainstorm the parts of a farm. Have them list things like: barn, house, fields, etc.

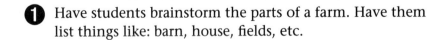

**②** Have students draw a picture of the farm they have described.

**③** Explain to students that they will be looking at pictures of a colonial farm plantation. As they tour the plantation, have students take note of differences between the plantations in colonial times and farms today.

**Mount Vernon Grounds Tour**
URL: http://www.mountvernon.org/education/grounds/

Students simply click on the pictures at this site to get a full screen picture. To continue the tour, the students need to click on the "Next" button at the bottom of each screen. The teacher may want to direct the students to click on the aerial view of Mount Vernon located on the first page of this site. [The teacher may also want the students to work in small groups at the computer.]

**④** Have students brainstorm all the differences they saw in the pictures of Mount Vernon from the farm they described in the beginning of the lesson.

**⑤** Group students into small working teams to design a plantation with all the different aspects of a colonial farm plantation. Have students include items like: main house, barns, carriage house, smoke house, etc.

 # Extensions

**①** Have students brainstorm how George Washington's daily home life was different from today's president. How is it similar? Draw a Venn diagram to illustrate the similarities and differences.

**②** Have students visit the White House to see how the president of the United States lives today.

**The White House Tour**
URL: http://www.whitehouse.gov/WH/Tours/White_House/

# A Virtual Tour of Betsy Ross's Home

## Overview

Betsy Ross is believed to be the creator of the first American flag commissioned by the Continental Congress. She is one of the most popular figures in American folklore. This virtual tour will help introduce students to Betsy and will help them better understand life during Revolutionary War times.

## Materials

- Computer with Internet access

## Objectives

- Take a virtual tour of the Betsy Ross house
- Explore Betsy's life during the Revolutionary War by examining the photos of her house

## Procedure

1 Ask the students to close their eyes and visualize the inside of their home. Have them imagine walking in the door. What do they see? Have them "walk" through various rooms of their house noticing decorations, things on the walls, things on tables, etc.

**2** Have them draw a picture of any room of their house. Have them be as detailed as possible. When completed, have them show and describe their room to the other students. After each student is done, have the other students tell you what they learned about that student. When they are all done, ask them whether there were any similarities to the drawings. Discuss with them why it is that many people have the same type of things. If someone a hundred years from now looked at one of their pictures, what would they learn about people who lived at this time?

**3** Tell the students that they are going to take a Cyberspace tour of a house from a long time ago. It is the house of Betsy Ross, the creator of the first American flag.

**Welcome to the Betsy Ross House**
URL: http://libertynet.org/iha/betsy/house/room1.html

As they tour the house, have them use the Lesson Plan Worksheet to guide them through the house. Have them note anything they learn about Betsy or life at the time of the Revolutionary War by looking at the pictures.

**4** Have each student share two things they learned about Betsy and life during the Revolutionary War from the tour.

# Extensions

**1** Have the students write a list of questions about Betsy Ross that seemed unanswered after the tour. Then read the stories of Betsy's life to the students to see if any of the questions were answered.

**The Story of Betsy Ross's Life**
URL: http://libertynet.org/iha/betsy/flaglife.html

**Betsy Ross and the American Flag**
URL: http://libertynet.org/iha/betsy/flagtale.html

**2** Have your students learn how to make a 5-pointed star with one snip of their scissors.

**How to Cut a 5-Pointed Star in One Snip**
URL: http://libertynet.org/iha/betsy/flagstar.html

# A Virtual Tour of Betsy Ross's Home

Student name: _____ Date: _____

**Directions:** Tour Betsy Ross's house to learn about her life and about life during the Revolutionary War.

**Welcome to the Betsy Ross House**
URL: http://libertynet.org/iha/betsy/house/room1.html

| Tour stop | What I learned about Betsy | What I learned about life during the Revolutionary War |
|---|---|---|
| Betsy Ross House Courtyard | | |
| The Kitchen | | |
| The Storage Room and the Cartridge Room | | |

**Activity Sheet**   A Virtual Tour of Betsy Ross's Home

| Tour stop | What I learned about Betsy | What I learned about life during the Revolutionary War |
|---|---|---|
| The Work Shop | | |
| Betsy's Bedroom | | |
| The Widow Lithgow's Bedroom | | |
| The Parlor | | |
| Betsy Memorabilia | | |

| LESSON PLAN |
| Number 7 |

# Old West Communities

## Overview

When the camera was invented in the late 1800s, it was used to document how the Wild West became organized communities. Students will be able to look at the photographs of the old West to imagine how these communities grew and changed over time.

## Objectives

- Use photographs to learn about life in old West communities and to examine how life in these communities has changed over time
- Recognize that various people may describe the same situation differently

## Procedure

**1** Have the students imagine a street in their community. Ask them how they think this street changed over time. What causes these changes? What would this street have looked like 100 years ago? Would it have been there?

**2** Explain to the students that they will be looking at some photos of streets and communities from the "Wild West." Have them go to the following Internet site:

**Photographs of the American West 1861-1912**
URL: http://gopher.nara.gov:70/0h/inform/dc/audvis/still/
        amwest.html

There is a section on this page titled "Towns out of Dust and Rock." Have the students scroll down to this section. Here they will find several jpeg images of communities in the old West. Have each student select one photograph to examine. They may want to look at a few before they make their selection. [Keep in mind that these images are fairly large, and it might take some time to download the students' selections.]

**3** Have the students use the accompanying worksheet to guide them in examining the photo (Photo #1 on the worksheet).

**4** Have the students examine a photo that was someone else's first choice. Direct the students to complete the worksheet for photo #2.

**5** Print out copies of each photo examined. Show each photo to the class. Have students who examined that particular photo share their impressions of the photo. Have a discussion about why the students think different people had different impressions of the same photo.

 # Extensions

**1** Use this Internet site to examine how people made a living in the 1800s.

**Photographs of the American West: 1861-1912**
URL: http://gopher.nara.gov:70/0h/inform/dc/audvis/still/
        amwest.html

Use the photographs from the following sections:

Bonanzas from the Earth
Life by the Sea
Life from the Land

After viewing the photographs from the various sections, have the students write a paragraph explaining which line of work they would have chosen if they lived at that time, and why.

# Old West Communities

**Student name:** _____    **Date:** _____

**Directions:** Use the photographs of the "Wild West" at the following Web site, then answer these questions.

**Photographs of the American West 1861-1912**
URL: http://gopher.nara.gov:70/0h/inform/dc/audvis/still/amwest.html

1. What is the most important thing you saw in the photo?

My photo:

_____

_____

My classmate's photo:

_____

_____

2. Tell two things about the photo that surprised you.

My photo:

_____

_____

**Activity Sheet**   Old West Communities
................................................................................

My classmate's photo:

_____

_____

3. Find and list two things in the photo that you might not see if the photo were taken today.

My photo:

_____

_____

My classmate's photo:

_____

_____

4. Give the photo a title which does a good job of describing the photo.

My photo:

_____

_____

My classmate's photo:

_____

_____

# White House Pets

 ## Overview

Many people have pets who share their homes like members of the family, but when you live in the White House, can your pet live there, too? This lesson will introduce your students to some of the famous "First Pets."

 ## Materials

- Computer with Internet access
- Crayons and pencils

 ## Objectives

- Name some famous First Pets
- Describe their antics
- Create an imaginary First Pet

 ## Procedure

**1** Ask your students if a pet may live in the White House. See if they can name a pet presently residing there. Introduce them to Socks, the Clintons' cat, by visiting this location from the White House for Kids.

**Pets in the White House**
http://www.whitehouse.gov/WH/kids/html/pets.html

**2** Have your students examine the pictures of the pets and read the paragraphs beside them. Have them answer questions as you read. Is Socks the first cat to live in the White House? Who was Old Whiskers? Who was the most famous and best loved of all First Pets? With what pets did Caroline Kennedy share the White House? What famous pet has written a book? Have your class name some of the funny things these pets have done.

**3** When you have finished, ask your students what pets they might have in the White House. Listen to their suggestions. Have them think about just one pet and imagine how it would look. Then pass out the activity sheets for this lesson. Each student may create his or her own First Pet in the box provided. Have them answer or help them answer the questions below their pictures. Display their imaginary First Pets.

# Extensions

**1** If you are interested in visiting real kids who have pets online, try this site. Have your students write their funny pet stories and send them to these friends.

**PETSTATION KIDS!**
URL: http://petstation.com/kids.html

**2** Many of the pets of the White House have belonged to children. To learn about kids who have lived in the White House, go to this site.

**Kids in the White House**
URL: http://www.whitehouse.gov/WH/kids/html/
        children.html

# White House Pets

**Student name:** _____  **Date:** _____

**Directions**: Think of a White House pet that you'd like to have. Imagine how it would look. Think of a name for your First Pet, and all the things that your First Pet would do in the White House. Complete the sentences below and then draw a picture of your First Pet on the other side of this page.

My First Pet's name is:

At the White House, my First Pet would:

**Activity Sheet**   White House Pets

# My First Pet

# Tour the White House

## Overview

Thousands of people visit the White House every year, but you can go there without stepping onto a school bus. In this lesson, your students will travel to the White House, via the Internet, to discover some of its history and take a virtual tour of its most notable rooms.

## Materials

- Computer with CD-ROM drive and iCD
- Paper and pencils
- Shoebox for each group of students
- Glue and scissors
- Paper and fabric scraps

## Objectives

- Recognize some of the rooms of the White House
- Explain some of its history
- Design a new room for the White House
- Work cooperatively in groups

## Procedure

**1** Begin by reading the history of the White House from this site. How was this site chosen for the President's house?

Who was the first President to live in the White House? How did it get its name?

**The History of the White House**
URL: http://www.whitehouse.gov/WH/kids/html/pre_his.html

**2** Take a tour of the White House. Have your class look at the picture of each room and read the description. Take special note of the President's Oval Office.

**The House-Tour**
URL: http://www.whitehouse.gov/WH/kids/html/tour.html

**3** Your students should now be familiar with some of the famous rooms of the White House. Allow them to work in small groups to design a new room for it. They may draw their ideas on paper and then make dioramas using art materials. When they are completed, put their "rooms" on display.

 # Extensions

**1** To get your students involved in the political scene, acquaint them with their President and Vice President. There is plenty of information here to share about our leaders and their wives.

**Our President**
URL: http://www.whitehouse.gov/WH/kids/html/couples.html

**2** An extension related to map reading is Where is the White House? This location has a map that gives not only where to find the White House, but also other monuments.

**Where is the White House?**
URL: http://www.whitehouse.gov/WH/kids/html/where.html

# Communities: Past and Present

 ## Overview

Students will begin exploring how communities have changed over time. Students will view past and present pictures of Philadelphia and determine how the community has changed over time.

 ## Materials

- Computer with Internet access

 ## Objectives

- Identify features of communities
- Identify how communities change over time
- Compare two photos of a community, past and present
- Draw a representation of their community, past and present

## Procedure

**Teacher's Note:** Before you begin this lesson, you should introduce a few concepts to students. Make sure that students can define and explain the following items: community; time relations - past, present, future; and features of a community.

**1** Ask the students to brainstorm all the features of a community. List those features on the board. Next ask the students to imagine that they lived more than a 100 years ago. What would their community look like? Tell them that they will investigate how one community changed over the years.

**2** Have the students work in small groups of three or four. One student in the group should serve as the recorder. Tell students that as investigators, they must generate as many features as possible about the community of Philadelphia from the photos that they will view on the Internet. Their job is to compare the photos and describe how the community has changed over time.

**3** Tell students to open the following Internet site:

**Philadelphia**
URL: http://libertynet.org/iha/postcards/hd2.html

**4** Pass out Worksheet #1 to the groups and review each question before the students begin this activity.

**5** When the groups have completed Worksheet #1, have them discuss the answers that they found with the class.

**6** After the discussion, have the groups open this next Web site:

**Philadelphia**
URL: http://libertynet.org/iha/postcards/phil1.html

Pass out Worksheet #2, review the questions with the class, and then have each group answer the questions.

**7** After the students have completed Worksheet #2, lead the class in a discussion about the changes that they observed. Ask your class to compare the two photos using the following questions to begin the discussion:

- In what ways were the two photos similar?
- In what ways did the community change?
- Name something that was in the first photo that was not seen in the second photo.

**8** As a culminating activity, have students draw pictures of their community. Have them divide the paper into halves. Instruct students to draw what they think their community looked like long ago on one side of the paper. On the other, have them draw a picture of their community as it is today.

 # Extensions

**1** Have students view some of the other photographs and postcards that are included at this site. Have students create their own community postcard that depicts some major site in a community or their own community.

**2** Have students design their own community. Give students graph paper to plot out roads and buildings. They should include government buildings, schools, homes, etc.

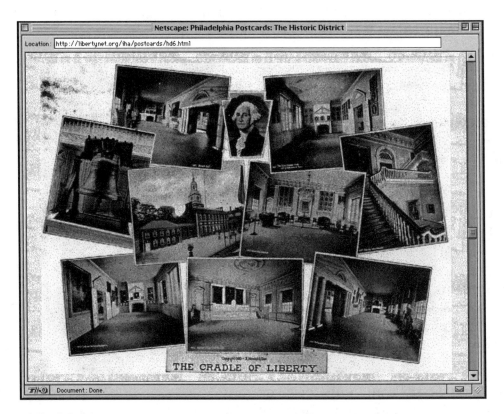

**Philadelphia**
URL: http://libertynet.org/iha/postcards/hd2.html

**Lesson Plan** Communities: Past and Present

Teaching American History with the Internet

# Communities: Past and Present

Activity Sheet 1

Student name: _____    Date: _____

1. What do you think are the most important things in the photo?

_____

_____

_____

2. What surprised you most in the photo?

_____

_____

_____

3. Find at least two things in the photo that might not be in a community of today.

_____

_____

_____

4. Give the photo a title that accurately describes its contents.

_____

**Activity Sheet**  Communities: Past and Present

# Communities: Past and Present

Activity Sheet 2

**Student name:** _____ **Date:** _____

1. Name some ways that the community has changed over time.

_____

_____

_____

_____

2. What do you think is the most important thing in this photo? Why?

_____

_____

_____

_____

3. What surprised you about the photo?

_____

_____

_____

4. Give the photo a title that accurately describes its contents.

_____

**Activity Sheet** Communities: Past and Present

# American History
## *Grades 4-6*

# Examining
# 200-Year-Old Documents

## Overview

Students will examine a 200-year-old document by Thomas Paine. Students will also discover information about old documents, primary resources, and printing processes of that period.

## Materials

- Computer with Internet access

## Objectives

- Identify aspects of old documents
- Identify purpose of *"Common Sense"* by Thomas Paine
- Identify terms associated with printing process and reporting

## Procedure

**1** Tell students that they will be examining documents that are over 200 years old. This lesson can tie in with a unit on Colonial America and Revolutionary America. Have students open the following Internet site:

**How to read a 200-Year-Old Document**
URL: http://www.earlyamerica.com./earlyamerica/howto.html

**②** This site will supply students with information about colonial documents. Pass out the worksheet called "Reading a 200-year-old Document" and have students work in pairs or small groups to answer the questions. The questions require students to identify aspects of old documents as well as associated terms. When students have completed the work have them share their answers with the rest of the class.

Explain to the students that they will put their new skills as curators to work and read an historic document.

**③** Students should open the following Internet site:

**Common Sense: The 1791 Bradford Edition of Thomas Paine's Common Sense**
URL: http://www.earlyamerica.com./earlyamerica/milestones/
commonsense/index.html

**④** Pass out the worksheet called "Common Sense." Students will examine Paine's "Common Sense" for the attributes of old documents noted in the last activity. Students need to click on each icon to get a full screen enlargement of the text of Paine's work. Have students share their results once they have completed the paper.

**Teacher's note**: You will need to define "propaganda" for your students before beginning this lesson.

 # Extensions

**①** Have students explore other important historic documents at the following Internet site:

**Milestone Historic Documents**
URL: http://www.earlyamerica.com/earlyamerica/milestones/
index.html

Have students work in pairs and explore a specific document and prepare a presentation to the class on their document.

**2** Have students write their own historic document. Remember to change the "s" to an "f".

**3** Make a paper into parchment. Before writing on it, dip one sheet at a time into a pan of tea and cool water. Leave it in the solution for 10 seconds and then lay it flat and let it air dry. It should turn a brownish yellow and wrinkle a bit.

**Common Sense: The 1791 Bradford Edition of Thomas Paine's Common Sense**
URL: http://www.earlyamerica.com./earlyamerica/milestones/commonsense/index.html

# Reading a 200-Year-Document

**Student name:** _____

**Date:** _____

1. Why is it difficult to read some words with the letter "S" in it? For what reason did printers use the letter substitute?

   _____

   _____

   _____

   _____

2. What is a primary source? Give one example.

   _____

   _____

   _____

3. Why are many 200-year-old documents in good condition?

_____

_____

_____

_____

4. How did printers set type in the colonial days?

_____

_____

_____

_____

5. What is meant by the following terms: browning and foxing ?

_____

_____

_____

_____

_____

**Activity Sheet**  Reading a 200-Year-Document

# Common Sense

**Student name:** _____

**Date:** _____

1. Find an example in the document where the letter "S" was substituted with the letter "F."

   _____

   _____

   _____

2. Why is this considered a primary source?

   _____

   _____

   _____

   _____

   _____

3. What did Thomas Paine call for in this document?

   _____

   _____

   _____

4. Why is Paine considered a propagandist?

_____

_____

_____

_____

_____

5. How would you describe Thomas Paine?

_____

_____

_____

_____

_____

6. What major event happened as a result of this document?

_____

_____

_____

_____

_____

# The United States Constitution

## Overview

This lesson will introduce students to some basic aspects of the United States Constitution. Students will look at the checks and balance system, how to amend the Constitution, liberties guaranteed in the Constitution, and the Bill of Rights.

## Materials

- Computer with Internet access

## Objectives

- Identify aspects of the United States Constitution
- Identify parts of the Constitution
- Identify the three branches of government
- Identify steps to amend the Constitution

## Procedure

1. This lesson will require some background information. You may want to introduce a little history surrounding the writing of the Constitution and the goals for writing the document. Then have students connect to the following Internet site:

**Vote-Smart—The Constitution**
URL: http://www.vote-smart.org/reference/primer/consti.html

This site will provide students with an easy-to-understand introduction to the United States Constitution.

**2** Pass out the worksheet for this lesson. The worksheet requires students to identify aspects of the United States Constitution, parts of the Constitution, the three branches of government, and the steps needed to amend the Constitution.

**3** Have students work in pairs to complete the activity and then have them share their answers with the rest of the class.

**4** A vocabulary list is provided at the end of the site. You can use it to assess the students' understanding.

 # Extensions

**1** Have students write a news report to inform the citizens about the separation of powers. Use this site to gather information:

**From Revolution to Reconstruction**
URL: http://grid.let.rug.nl/~welling/usa/revolution.html

Students should click on the following link: "The formation of a national government." Then have them click on "Leaders favor separation of power."

**2** Create your own government in class. Write a constitution with a bill of rights. Allow students to make amendments using the method already established by the U.S. government.

# The United States Constitution

**Student name:** _____

**Date:** _____

1. Name the three branches of government.

Three branches:

_____

_____

_____

Give 2 ways that each branch can check another branch.

Congress:

_____

_____

President:

_____

_____

Courts:

_____

_____

2. Name three liberties guaranteed by the Constitution.

1. _____

2. _____

3. _____

3. What is the Bill of Rights?

_____

_____

_____

4. Which amendment do you think is most important and why?

_____

_____

_____

5. In what two ways can an amendment be proposed?

_____

_____

_____

6. How can an amendment be ratified?

_____

_____

**Activity Sheet** The United States Constitution

7. How many amendments have been ratified by Congress?

_____

_____

_____

_____

8. Define the following terms:

Executive Order

_____

Impeachment

_____

Habeus Corpus

_____

Ex Post Facto Law

_____

Double Jeopardy

_____

Bill of Attainer

_____

# Overview

Students will work with Internet sites and activities designed to help them better understand how a bill becomes a law.

 # Materials

- Computer with Internet access
- Classroom copies of lesson plan worksheets

Objectives

- Identify the process through which a bill goes to becomes a law
- Define terms associated with this process

Procedure

**1** Establish or review background information for this lesson. Make sure that all students understand the following items: division of powers; two houses of Congress; and why we create and need laws.

**❷** Once this background has been established have students begin this lesson by connecting to the following Internet site:

**Vote-Smart-How a Bill Becomes a Law**
URL: http://www.vote-smart.org/reference/primer/billlaw.html

This site gives an excellent, clear, concise introduction into how a bill becomes a law. Pass out the worksheet. You may want to have students work in pairs or triads to complete the activity. The worksheet covers the process by which a bill becomes a law and require students to define terms associated with the process. Once students have completed this activity have them share their findings with the rest of the class.

**❸** Have students brainstorm possible bills that they feel should be submitted to Congress to become laws. Have them submit them to the rest of the class for discussion and revision.

**❹** Call your local representative to schedule a visit so that they may discuss the law making process. Prep students with questions before the visit. Have students ask the representatives about such topics as: bills they have submitted; bills they were against; how many times a year they vote on bills; committees they serve on, etc.

**❺** Then have students share some of the bills they created as a classroom and have the congress person share their ideas on what the students have proposed.

 # Extensions

**❶** Students can gain a more in-depth look at how a bill becomes a law by opening the following Internet site:

**The Library of Congress**
URL: http://thomas.loc.gov/home/lawsmade.toc.html

Break students into groups to explore and report on the various parts of the law making process.

**❷** Take a tour of the U.S. Capitol
URL: http://www.senate.gov/capitol/virtour.html

# How a Bill Becomes a Law

**Student name:** _____  **Date:** _____

1. Describe briefly how legislation is introduced.

_____

_____

_____

_____

_____

2. Read the steps involved when a committee receives a bill. After reading the eight steps, summarize, in your own words, what the committee does with a bill in two sentences.

_____

_____

_____

_____

_____

3. What happens when a bill is placed on the calendar?

_____

_____

_____

_____

_____

4. What happens during the debate period?

_____

_____

_____

_____

_____

5. What happens to the bill if it is passed when voted on?

_____

_____

_____

6. What is the Conference Committee?

_____

_____

_____

7. What three options does the President have when a bill reaches his office?

_____

_____

_____

# Terms to Define

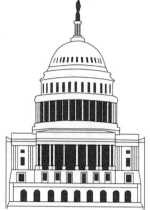

Student name: _____

Date: _____

1. Public Bill -

_____

_____

2. Filibuster -

_____

_____

3. Hopper -

_____

_____

4. Sponsor -

_____

_____

5. Veto -

_____

_____

# The Boston Tea Party

## Overview

This lesson will introduce students to the Boston Tea Party. Students will use the Internet to access information about the event and complete two activities.

## Materials

- Computer with Internet access
- Crayons or markers

## Objectives

- Identify what happened at the Boston Tea Party
- Identify why colonists participated in the Boston Tea Party

## Procedure

**Teacher's Note:** Students will need some background information about Colonial America at this period in time. Students should be aware of the following ideas: taxation without representation; growing resentments towards English rule; and England's trade monopoly.

**1** Have students open the following Internet site:

**The Boston Tea Party**
URL: http://grid.let.rug.nl/~welling/usa/revolution.html

Students should click on the link "The War of Independence," and then on the link titled "Patriots Agitate: The Boston Tea Party." Students will use this site and the "Boston Harbor" site to complete the first activity.

**2** Have students read the account of the Boston Tea Party online. When they get to the bottom of the first account, have them click on the link called "Boston Harbor". That link is highlighted at the end of the passage.

**3** Once they have finished reading the accounts, pass out the worksheet called "Join Us For Tea." Have students write a proclamation that would be posted in the marketplace for other colonists to read. It is a secret invitation to join the Boston Tea Party rebels. Students should include reasons to attend the party.

**4** After they have completed their proclamation, have them draw a picture of the Boston Tea Party. Students then share their proclamations and drawings with the rest of the class.

 # Extensions

**1** Students may not realize that the Boston Tea Party was not the only time tea was dumped into the water in protest. Students may want to learn about the New York Tea Party and compare that event to the Boston Tea Party. Have students use the following Internet site to gain information on the New York Tea Party:

**The War for Independence — Town and Country Magazine, June 1774**
URL: http://home.ptd.net/~revwar/town.html

# Join Us For Tea

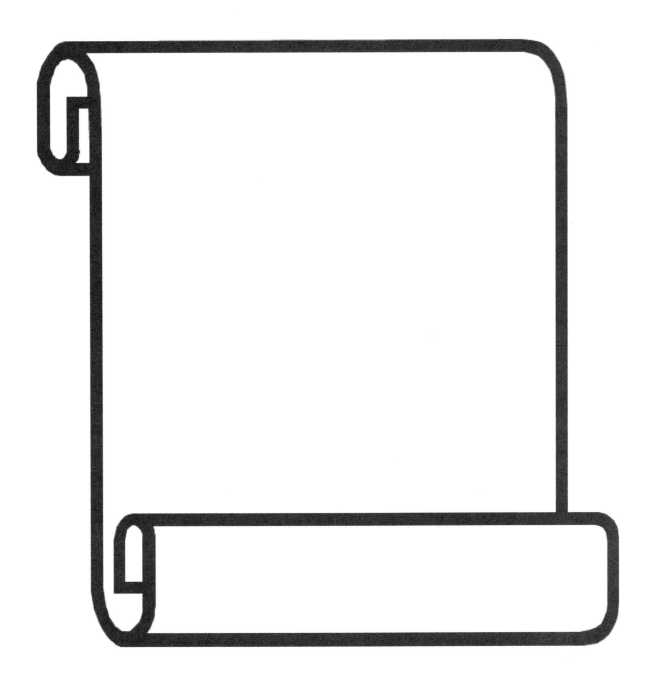

# You Were There

**Student name:** _____ **Date:** _____

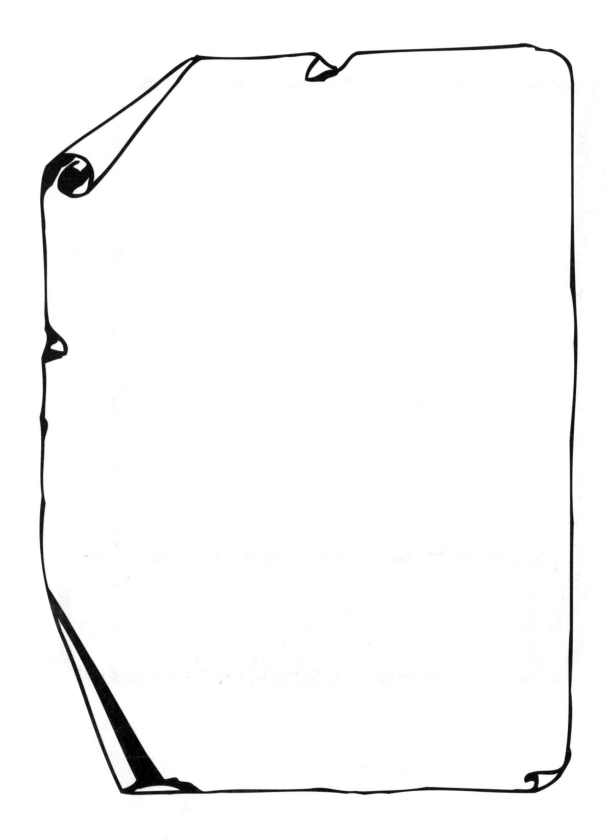

# The Underground Railroad

 ## Overview

Students will examine information about the underground railroad and identify reasons for its existence and the importance of the role it played during the Civil War period.

 ## Materials

- Computer with Internet access

## Objectives

- Identify organization and origins of the underground railroad
- Examine information about slavery in the Western Hemisphere
- Identify facts about runaway slaves and the abolition movement

## Procedure

Teachers will need to establish background information for students before beginning this lesson. Students should be aware of the following concepts:

- slavery in the South
- growing abolitionist's movement

- slavery conditions (selling, runaways, etc.)
- South's dependency on slavery for labor

Once students have this initial background, begin this lesson. Students will examine the topic of the underground railroad. Students need to connect to the following Internet site:

**History and Geography of the Underground Railroad**
URL: http://www.nps.gov/undergroundrr/history.htm

This site will provide for the understanding of a number of issues surrounding the underground railroad.

Divide your class into groups of five students. Each group will be responsible for summarizing a part of the article and sharing the information with the rest of the group. Have students within each group number themselves off. Each number will correspond to a section of the activity and the article on the Internet. Pass out the lesson plan worksheets.

At this point have all the ones break into a new group, the twos into a group, the threes, and so on. The ones will be responsible for summarizing the information in the first section, the twos about the second section, etc. Once students have completed the activity, have them return to their original groups and share their findings with the rest of the group. In this manner each student will get a complete picture of the information provided in the article. Complete the activity by conducting a classroom discussion of the topic.

 # Extensions

 To help students further understand the Underground Railroad, have them read . . . *If You Traveled on The Underground Railroad* by Ellen Levine.

# The Underground Railroad

**Student name:** _____ **Date:** _____

#1 Introduction

Summarize the introduction for the rest of your group.

_____

_____

_____

_____

_____

_____

_____

_____

_____

_____

_____

_____

**Activity Sheet**  The Underground Railroad

Summarize this section for the rest of your group.

_____

_____

_____

_____

_____

_____

_____

_____

_____

_____

_____

_____

_____

_____

_____

_____

_____

**Activity Sheet**   The Underground Railroad

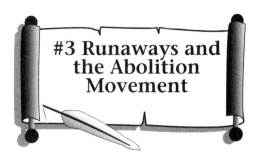

# #3 Runaways and the Abolition Movement

Summarize this section for the rest of your group.

_____

_____

_____

_____

_____

_____

_____

_____

_____

_____

_____

_____

_____

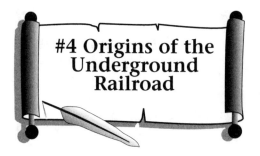

# #4 Origins of the Underground Railroad

Summarize this section for the rest of your group.

_____

_____

_____

_____

_____

_____

_____

_____

_____

_____

_____

_____

_____

_____

_____

_____

_____

**Activity Sheet**   The Underground Railroad

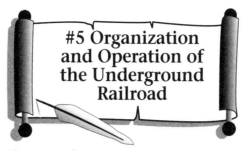

# #5 Organization and Operation of the Underground Railroad

Summarize this section for the rest of your group.

_____

_____

_____

_____

_____

_____

_____

_____

_____

_____

_____

_____

_____

_____

_____

_____

**Activity Sheet**   The Underground Railroad

# Western Folklore

## Overview

This lesson will introduce students to some of the Western lore that has been handed down through generations. Students will learn the story of young Willie Keil and the story of how he helped save hundreds of lives.

## Materials

- Computer with Internet access

## Objectives

- Identify dangers of traveling West, and reasons people had for moving West through completion of a journal entry
- Read a story about one group of people and their journey West

## Procedure

**1** The teacher should supply students with background information about the Western Expansion. (You may want to read part of the article "Literature and the Frontier," URL: http://let.rug.n1) Brainstorm with your students about why people moved West: to stake a gold claim, to settle on free or low-cost land, to escape the Civil War, or for religious reasons. Students should also be made aware that the government supported and created incentives to help people move West so that the land would be settled. It was felt that if the lands were settled from coast to coast that America was less likely to be invaded or have another country claim the land as their own. Students should also be informed about jumping-off points and trails such as the Oregon Trail as well as the tremendous hardships that the pioneers faced when moving West. Many people moving West died as a result of illness, disease, weather, or Indians.

**2** Once students have this background, have them begin this lesson by opening the following Internet site:

**The History Net—Willie Keil Saved Lives on the Long Journey West . . . Even Though He was Dead**
URL: http://www.thehistorynet.com/WildWest/articles/
08963_text.htm

This will connect students to the story of Willie Keil and his father. Willie is credited with saving the lives of approximately 200 people that went on the journey with him. What makes the story even more interesting is that Willie did this while he was dead. Had Willie not died before the journey, the group of two hundred would probably have been killed by Indians.

**3** Have students read this fascinating story about Willie and use the accompanying worksheet to write a journal about the reasons that motivated people to travel West and the dangers associated with these journeys. Once students have completed the work, have them discuss the story with the rest of the class or in small discussion groups.

# Extensions

**1** Have students write a story about traveling West in a Conestoga Wagon. Students can gain information about a Conestoga Wagon at the following internet site:

**Conestoga Wagon**
URL: http://vd1.magibox.net/lonesome_turkey/support/
html/conestoga.html

This site will give students a picture and description of the Conestoga Wagon which was used to travel West during the Westward expansion in the United States.

# Westward Ho Journal

**Student name:** _____  **Date:** _____

Write a journal entry as if you were moving West with Keil's group. Make sure to include the reasons for travelling West, and about the dangers you face.

*May 1855*

# Westward Expansion

 ## Overview

After receiving background information about the Westward Expansion in American history, students will read personal accounts of the hardships faced in the Midwest. Students will then write an essay explaining a topic that summarizes an historical account.

 ## Materials

- Computer with Internet access
- Classroom copies of lesson plan worksheets

## Objectives

- Identify facts about the Westward expansion
- Identify information about the time period through primary sources
- Demonstrate comprehension through completing an essay explaining a topic that summarizes an historical account.

 ## Procedure

**1** Have students connect to the following Internet site: From Revolution to Reconstruction:

**Westward Expansion and Regional Differences—
Literature and Frontier**
URL: `http://www.let.rug.nl/~welling/usa/revolution.html`

Students need to scroll down to click on the link "Westward Expansion and Regional Differences". Then have students select the link "Literature and Frontier". This site provides students with information about the Westward Expansion. The information actually begins on paragraph four of the text. Have students read the information.

**❷** Once the students have read the material, have them write an essay on one of the following topics:
- Look up the definition of "frontier" and explain how the name reflects on the area.
- Explain the reasons why people chose to move to the frontier.
- Explain why the settlers of the frontier were called emmigrants and not immigrants

**❸** After the essay assignment is completed, have students open the following Internet site:

**Mark Detleu Hauberg**
URL: http://www.augustana.edu/library/mhauberg.html

This site provides students with a first-hand account of a farmer's perspective on this time. Have students read this account. Then have students open the next site:

**Emma Oltman**
URL: http://www.augustana.edu/library/oltman.html

This site provides students with an account from Emma Oltman during the later part of the Westward Expansion. She recounts earlier times of the expansion period. Have students read her account.

**❹** Once students have read both accounts, have them complete the accompanying worksheet. Have students draft letters to either Mark Hauberg or Emma Oltman. In the letters, the students must comment on what they read and ask questions as if Mark or Emma was still alive. Students could then use their questions to start researching other aspects of the Westward Expansion.

# Extensions

**1** Have students explore the California gold rush by opening the following Internet site:

**Mindscape: California Gold Rush**
URL: http://www.mindscape.com/reference/california/
 gold.html

Have students write a play about the California gold rush based upon the information they research. Be sure that they include the "who, what, when, where, how, and why" of the Gold Rush.

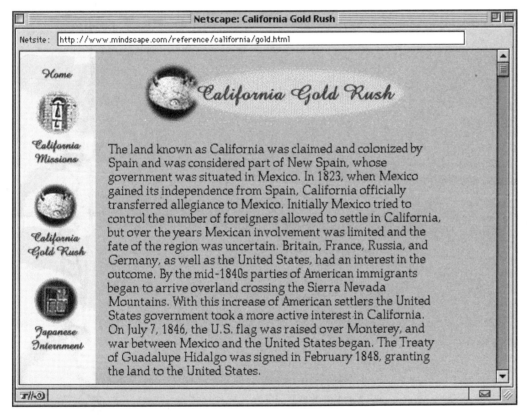

Netscape: California Gold Rush

Netsite: http://www.mindscape.com/reference/california/gold.html

*Home*

*California Missions*

*California Gold Rush*

*Japanese Internment*

## California Gold Rush

The land known as California was claimed and colonized by Spain and was considered part of New Spain, whose government was situated in Mexico. In 1823, when Mexico gained its independence from Spain, California officially transferred allegiance to Mexico. Initially Mexico tried to control the number of foreigners allowed to settle in California, but over the years Mexican involvement was limited and the fate of the region was uncertain. Britain, France, Russia, and Germany, as well as the United States, had an interest in the outcome. By the mid-1840s parties of American immigrants began to arrive overland crossing the Sierra Nevada Mountains. With this increase of American settlers the United States government took a more active interest in California. On July 7, 1846, the U.S. flag was raised over Monterey, and war between Mexico and the United States began. The Treaty of Guadalupe Hidalgo was signed in February 1848, granting the land to the United States.

**Mindscape: California Gold Rush**
URL: http://www.mindscape.com/reference/california/gold.html

# Westward Expansion Letter

Student name: _____   Date: _____

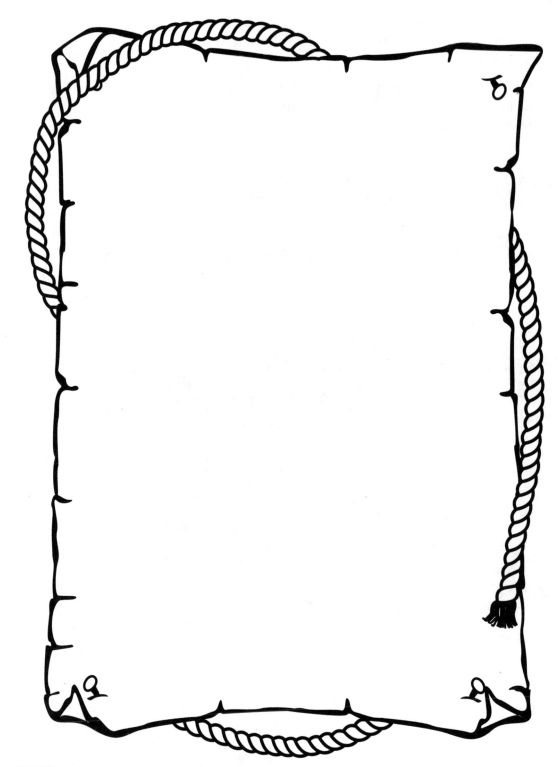

**Activity Sheet**   Westward Expansion

74

## LESSON PLAN

### Number 8

# The Industrial Revolution: Lesson One

## Overview

This lesson will introduce students to Rebecca Pennock who lived during the Industrial Revolution. Students will read how Rebecca took over her late husband's iron mill on the Brandywine River in Pennsylvania and built it into a company called Lukens Steel.

## Materials

- Computer with Internet access
- Paper, markers, stapler

## Objectives

- Identify facts about the Industrial Revolution
- Read the story about Rebecca Pennock and Luken's Steel
- Participate in a simulation assembly line
- Identify reasons for assembly line manufacturing

## Procedure

**1** Give students some background information on the Industrial Revolution. Establish the following understanding with your students:

- Rise of Industry in the North
- Reasons for the Industrial Revolution
- Industrial Magnets (J. P. Getty, Rockefeller)
- Social problems that arose as a result of the Industrial Revolution

**2** Once you have established this background information, have students engage in the following simulation to help them understand how labor had changed in America at this time. The activity will require a little preparation before you start the lesson.

## Simulation

1. Break students into small groups of five students each, and select a few students who would be willing to work on their own.

2. Tell students that they will be making bowling bags to be sold for a profit. As the teacher, you will be buying only bags from the group that makes the most and has the best quality. You will have the right to reject any bag(s) or company that does not produce high quality material in large quantities.

3. Show students the attached prototype bag that their small company will be making.

4. Students should be instructed in how to make the bag. Tell students that each bag must have the company logo written on it before it is finished. Tell students that they will need to divide their group up to work cooperatively in making the bags. Each student will need to complete a part of the project.

5. One of the students in each group (company) should be selected as quality control. They have the right to reject any bag that they feel does not meet the standard necessary for sales.

6. Allow five minutes for each group to organize their supplies and themselves before beginning the project.

7. After the project time is up, count the number of products and determine which group will be award the contract and money for their bags.

8. Once the project is complete, have students discuss the process they just went through in producing the product. Discuss the following items:

- Who made the most and why?

- What happened to the quality of the product?

- What are the reasons for using an assembly line?

**❸** Lead the discussion about the move toward assembly lines in business and the growth of big business. Then have students open to the following Internet site:

**The History Net—Industrial**
URL: http://www.thehistorynet.com/AmericanHistory/
articles/0495_text.htm

This site will connect students to the story of Rebecca Pennock and Lukens Steel Industry. Have students read the material and complete the accompanying worksheet. Once students have completed this work have them share their results with the rest of the class.

 # Extensions

**❶** Have students further explore the problems of city life that were produced by the Industrial Revolution by opening the following Internet site:

**How the Other Half Lives: Studies Among the Tenements of New York**
URL: http://www.cis.yale.edu/amstud/inforev/riis/title.html

**Teacher's Note:** This site is a 5th grade & up reading level.

# The Industrial Revolution: Lesson One

**Student name:** _____

**Class:** _____ **Date:** _____

Each part of the bag needs to be cut out, the handle glued or stapled, and the label written on the front of the bag.

Each bag must say "Fun Bags Incorporated."

The print should be neat, colorful, and easy to read.

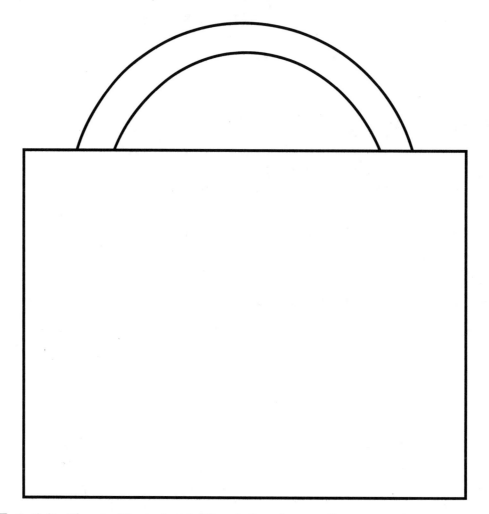

**Activity Sheet** The Industrial Revolution: Lesson One

# Lukens Steel Industry

**Student name:** _____

**Class:** _____ **Date:** _____

1. Describe Rebecca (Pennock) Lukens as an individual.

   _____

   _____

   _____

2. Name some products that used Lukens Steel.

   _____

   _____

   _____

3. How did Rebecca help to turn around Lukens Steel?

   _____

   _____

   _____

4. Why do you think that Rebecca's family was not happy about her running the business?

   _____

   _____

   _____

# The Industrial Revolution: Lesson Two

## Overview

This lesson will introduce students to the Industrial Revolution. Students will gain an understanding of some of the great industrial barons of the time and the problems that were developing in the cities as a result of the Industrial Revolution.

## Materials

- Computer with Internet access

## Objectives

- Describe this historical period
- Identify leaders of business at this time
- Identify consequences of the industrial growth

## Procedure

**1** Students should be aware that while civilization was moving toward an industrial culture, this movement was not necessarily global. Many nations, as well as many parts of the United States, were still grappling with the agricultural revolution at that time. It was this industrial growth in the North and the agricultural dependency in the

South that helped to contribute to the secession of states and eventually the Civil War.

**2** Have students open the following Internet site:

**From Revolution to Reconstruction**
URL: http://www.let.rug.nl/~welling/usa/revolution.html

This site connects students to information about the Industrial Revolution. They need to click on the site Industry Grows Bigger and Bigger.

**3** Pass out the accompanying worksheets to students and have them use them to understand the information presented on this site. The worksheets ask students to describe developments during this historical period, comment on industry leaders, and identify the consequences of industrial growth on the cities. When students reach the end of the first page of the site, instruct students to click on the right arrow at the bottom. This link will take students to the next page in the activity called: Cities and Problems Multiply.

**4** Pair students off for this activity. Have student pairs read the information on the two pages of this Web site. Then have students complete the work on the worksheet.

**5** Once students have completed the work have them share their work with the rest of the class.

 # Extensions

**1** Have students explore the problems in the cities at the turn of the century by opening the following Internet site:

**On The Lower East Side**
URL: http://140.190.128.190/SMC/Dept/history/Contents.html

Have students create a big book about the information they gather when researching.

# The Industrial Revolution
## Lesson Two

**Student name:** _____

**Class:** _____  **Date:** _____

Summarize the life of Andrew Carnegie in the space provided.

_____

_____

_____

_____

_____

_____

Describe other industrial developments during this period of time.

_____

_____

_____

_____

_____

_____

_____

**Activity Sheet**   The Industrial Revolution: Lesson Two

Why were cities growing at this time?

_____

_____

_____

_____

_____

_____

What was the Interstate Commerce Act?

_____

_____

_____

_____

_____

Why was Theodore Roosevelt nicknamed the "Trust-buster?

_____

_____

_____

_____

_____

**Activity Sheet** The Industrial Revolution: Lesson Two

| LESSON PLAN |
| Number 10 |

# Ellis Island: Lesson One

## Overview

This lesson will introduce students to European immigrants coming to America in the late 1800s. Students will gain information about Ellis Island and the immigrants' journey to America. Students will also examine photographs of the Ellis Island Immigration processing site.

## Material

• Computer with Internet access

## Objectives

• Identify facts about Ellis Island
• Identify purpose of Ellis Island
• Create empathy towards immigrants coming to America
• View photographs of Ellis Island

## Procedure

**1** Establish some background information for students on this topic. Make sure students understand information on the following topics:
  • Industrial revolution

- Basic problems in Europe at this time
- Promise of a better future in America

**❷** Explain to students that they will be examining information about Ellis Island over the next two or three days. Today they will be introduced to Ellis Island and they will view photographs of the Ellis Island Immigration Processing Station.

Have students open the following Internet site:

**Ellis Island: Overview**
URL: http://www.i-channel.com/ellis/overview.html

This site will take students to an overview of the Ellis Island Immigration Station. The sites used in this lesson have photos, text, and sound bites. Have students take advantage of all the information available on each page. Pass out the first accompanying activity sheet. Have students go through the site and complete the information on the sheet. The worksheet requires students to think about the facts related to Ellis Island. It also questions them on their feelings, promoting empathy for the immigrants. Students will also need to use the following site to complete the first activity sheet, Ellis Island:

**The Journey**
URL: http://www.i-channel.com/ellis/journey.html

Once students have completed the first worksheet have them share their results with the rest of the class.

**❸** Pass out the second activity sheet, and have students connect to the following Internet site:

**New York, NY, Ellis Island — Immigration: 1900-1920**
URL: http://cmp1.ucr.edu/exhibitions/immigration_id.html

This site connects students to a site that contains approximately 24 photographs of Ellis Island. Have students view the photographs. Have students write captions for at least four pictures of their choice. Students should write the captions from the view of the immigrants coming to America.

Teacher's Note: Students will need to click on the "next button" at the bottom of the screen to view the additional photographs. In addition, if students want to view a larger version of the photographs, have them simply click on the photo or description and a larger version of the photograph will be downloaded to your computer.

# Extensions

**❶** Students may want to view additional photographs of Ellis Island. Students can do this by opening the following Internet site:

**Ellis Island**
URL: http://www.TheInsider.com/NYC/Photos/Ellis.htm

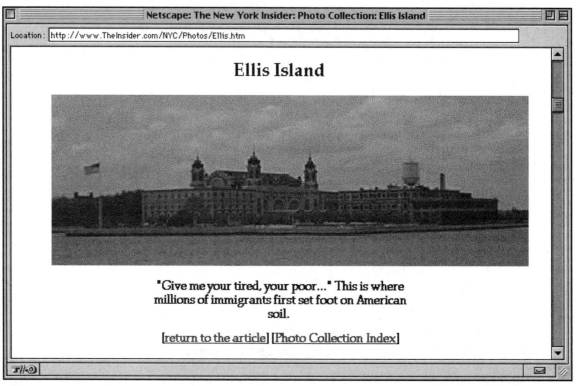

**Ellis Island**
URL: http://www.TheInsider.com/NYC/Photos/Ellis.htm

# Ellis Island

**Student name:** _____

**Class:** _____ **Date:** _____

1. How many immigrants were processed through Ellis Island?

_____

2. What symbolized a closing the door policy on immigrants?

_____

_____

_____

3. What happened to people that did not pass inspection?

_____

_____

_____

4. What is at Ellis Island today?

_____

_____

_____

5. Summarize what the Journey to America was like for many immigrants.

_____

_____

_____

_____

6. Download at least two sound clips and describe what you heard and your reaction to it.

_____

_____

_____

_____

7. What do you think it was like for the immigrants passing through the Ellis Island station?

_____

_____

_____

_____

8. How would you react to the inspections made at the Stations?

_____

_____

_____

_____

# Photograph
# Descriptions

**Student name:** _____

**Class:** _____  **Date:** _____

Directions: Choose four photographs and describe what you see and how you think the
immigrants felt in the picture.

Title

```
┌─────────────────────────────────────────────┐
│                                               │
│                                               │
│                                               │
│                                               │
│                                               │
└─────────────────────────────────────────────┘
```

Title

```
┌─────────────────────────────────────────────┐
│                                               │
│                                               │
│                                               │
│                                               │
│                                               │
└─────────────────────────────────────────────┘
```

Title

```
┌─────────────────────────────────────────────┐
│                                               │
│                                               │
│                                               │
│                                               │
│                                               │
└─────────────────────────────────────────────┘
```

Title

```
┌─────────────────────────────────────────────┐
│                                               │
│                                               │
│                                               │
│                                               │
│                                               │
└─────────────────────────────────────────────┘
```

# Ellis Island: Lesson Two

## Overview

This lesson is a continuation of Ellis Island: Part 1. In this lesson, students will take a closer look at the immigrants' experiences at the Ellis Island Processing Station.

## Material

- Computer with Internet access

## Objectives

- Identify processing procedures for immigrants
- Identify the feelings of many immigrants going through this process
- View photographs of Ellis Island
- Listen to immigrant sound clips

## Procedure

**1** You can use Ellis Island: Part 1 as the background for this lesson. In this lesson students will examine the processing of immigrants in more depth. To accomplish this activity, students will move back and forth through a number of Web pages that are linked.

❷ Have students open the following Internet site:

**Ellis Island: Processing**
URL: http://www.i-channel.com/ellis/process.html

This Web page describes Ellis Island processing procedures. At the bottom of this page are six additional links on which students need to click in order to complete the activity.

Teacher's Note: When students are finished with the page they simply need to click on the "back" button at the top of their menu bar to go back to the other links.

❸ Pass out the accompanying worksheet for the students to complete. At the Web site, students can explore the various media, including sound clips, text, and photographs.

❹ Here is a list of individual URLs in case you want to use the sites separately.

**Arrival**
URL: http://www.i-channel.com/ellis/arrival.html

**Medical**
URL: http://www.i-channel.com/ellis/medical.html

**Mental**
URL: http://www.i-channel.com/ellis/mental.html

**Legal Inspection**
URL: http://www.i-channel.com/ellis/legal.html

**Detention**
URL: http://www.i-channel.com/ellis/detention.html

**Free to Land**
URL: http://www.i-channel.com/ellis/free.html

 # Extensions

**1** Have students examine Ellis Island as it is today. Students can gain this information by opening the following Internet site:

**Ellis Island Today**
URL: http://www.i-channel.com/ellis/today.html

Students will be able to explore photos and text about the restoration of the Ellis Island Processing Station.

**Arrival**
URL: http://www.i-channel.com/ellis/arrival.html

# Ellis Island
# Processing

**Student name:** _____

**Class:** _____ **Date:** _____

1. How do the personal accounts of the immigrants help you to understand more about Ellis Island?

   _____

   _____

   _____

2. Download one of the sound clips and describe the information you hear.

   _____

   _____

   _____

3. Describe the conditions when immigrants first reached Ellis Island.

   _____

   _____

   _____

4. Why would doctors chalk a letter on some immigrants' clothing lapels?

   _____

   _____

   _____

5. What were some of the marks that doctors would make on immigrants' clothing?

_____

_____

_____

6. What is "trachoma?"

_____

_____

_____

7. Name some ways that immigrants were tested for mental health.

_____

_____

_____

8. Why were some of these tests unfair?

_____

_____

_____

9. What is a "manifest sheet?"

_____

_____

10. What was thought to happen to many immigrant names at Ellis Island?

_____

_____

_____

**Activity Sheet** Ellis Island Processing

11. What does the phrase "Liable to become a Public Charge" mean?

_____

_____

_____

12. For what reason might women and children be detained at Ellis Island?

_____

_____

_____

13. For what reason did immigrants have tags pinned to their clothing?

_____

_____

_____

14. Choose two photographs and write a description for the picture.

_____

_____

_____

15. Download another sound clip and describe what you hear.

_____

_____

_____

# Vietnam War

## Overview

This lesson will introduce students to the Vietnam War through the eyes of a soldier. This gripping account will help students understand the magnitude of battle and the feelings and emotions of those going through the war.

## Materials

- Computer with Internet access

Objectives

- Identify aspects of the Vietnam War through personal soldier accounts
- Create empathy for the victims of war (both civilian and soldier)

## Procedure

❶ Establish some background information for the students before beginning this lesson. Students should be aware of the U.S. involvement in the war and the reasons the U.S. had for entering the conflict. Students should also be aware of the growing civilian resentment to the war in the U.S. Make students aware of the reaction many people had to soldiers returning from the war.

**❷** Once you have established some background knowledge for students on the Vietnam War, have them open the following Internet site:

**The History Net—Vietnam**
URL:
> http://www.thehistorynet.com/Vietnam/articles/12961_text.htm

This site will connect students to an article entitled "Trial by Fire," written by a Vietnam War soldier. Captain Thomas A. Pienta, U. S. Army (retired), wrote an account of the time he spent in Vietnam. The account is gripping and provides a clear picture of a Vietnam battle that left him injured and fellow soldiers dead. Captain Pienta paints a vivid picture of the events of the battle and his feelings and thoughts as the battle unfolded and he was injured.

**❸** Have students read the account and complete the accompanying worksheet. Students will examine the feelings of the soldiers, reading a first-hand account of what it is like to be a part of the battle, and what it meant to one person to have lost fellow soldiers in battle.

**❹** While reading the article, students should identify some of the feelings, thoughts, experiences, and memories the soldier recounted in his story, using the story Web: From the soldier's point of view.

**❺** Once students have completed this activity, have them complete it a second time. This time they should record their own feelings, thoughts, experiences, and memories about the soldier's experiences.

**❻** Then have students write a letter to Captain Thomas A. Pienta about his experience in battle. Have them put their own reactions to the material and questions they may ask of him if they ever get the chance. Have students share their work with the rest of the class.

# Extensions

❶ Have students express their feelings about Vietnam Combat Art. They can view the artwork at the following site:

**U. S. Army Vietnam Combat Art**
URL: http://members.aol.com/jimm844224/vietart1.html

**U. S. Army Vietnam Combat Art: Waiting to Lift Off**
URL: http://members.aol.com/jimm844224/vietart1.html

# Vietnam War

Student name: _____

Class: _____     Date: _____

**From the Soldier's Point of View**

Feelings:



Thoughts:



Experiences:



Memories:

| My Personal Reaction to the Story | Feelings: (As I read I felt . . . ) |
| --- | --- |
| | Thoughts: (I couldn't help thinking . . . ) |
| | Experiences: (reminds me of . . . ) |
| | Memories: (I will remember . . . ) |

**Activity Sheet**   Vietnam War

# Vietnam War

Student name: _____

Class: _____  Date: _____

## A Letter to Captain Thomas A. Pienta, U.S. Army (ret.)

_____

_____

_____

_____

_____

_____

_____

_____

_____

_____

_____

_____

# Appendix

## *American History Internet Resources*

# Newsgroups

**American Revolution/international perspectives.**
soc.history.war.us-revolution

**Aspects of the U.S. Civil War. (Moderated)**
soc.history.war.us-civil-war

**The Vietnam War. (Moderated)**
soc.history.war.vietnam

**History & events of World War Two. (Moderated)**
soc.history.war.world-war-ii

**Social Studies and History curriculum in K-12 education**
k12.ed.soc-studies

# E-mail discussion groups

**Teaching American History**
TAMHA

**Early American History Discussion Group**
HIST285

**"Help History Education Become More Hands-On"**
caerleon

**H-NET List for Women's History**
H-WOMEN

# WWW sites:

**Thomas Jefferson**
URL: http://www2.lucidcafe.com/lucidcafe/lucidcafe/
      library/96apr/jefferson.html

**Yahoo/Arts:Humanities:History**
URL: http://www.yahoo.com/arts/humanities/history/

**Women and History**
URL: http://www.city-net.com/~lmann/women/history/
    index.html

**Women's History in America**
URL: http://www.wic.org/misc/history.htm

**Links for United States History**
URL: http://www.sidwell.edu/%7Ejewell/us.html

**A Chronology of US Historical Documents**
URL: http://www.law.uoknor.edu/ushist.html

**United States History Research Page**
URL: http://members.aol.com/Docent1/ushist.htm

**The U.S. House of Representatives Internet Law Library**
URL: http://law.house.gov/8.htm

**U.S. HISTORICAL DOCUMENTS ARCHIVE**
URL: http://w3.one.net/%7Emweiler/ushda/ushda.htm

**Another United States History Links Page**
URL: http://we.got.net/docent/soquel/ushist.htm

**The American Revolution**
URL: http://www.tiac.net/users/flopes/

**National Standards for United States History**
URL: http://www.sscnet.ucla.edu/nchs/us-toc.htm

**SCORE History-Social Science**
URL: http://www.rims.k12.ca.us/score/index.html

**Revolutionary War Documents**
URL: http://www.uconect.net/~histnact/revwar/document.html

**Plymouth: It's History and People**
URL: http://media3.com/plymouth/history/index.htm

**Archives of Personal Experience and Related Resources**
URL: http://libertynet.org/%7Ezelson/publish/list.html#hist

**History/Social St8/ÄP8 @or K-12 Teac1å**
URL: http://www.execpc.com/~dboals/amer.html

## Nineteenth Century U.S.
URL: http://www.msstate.edu/Archives/History/
USA/19th_C./nineteen.html

## Primary Sources on the Internet--The Federal Writers Project
URL: http://www.sidwell.edu/%7Ejewell/newdeal.html

## Native American History Archives
URL: http://library.ccsu.ctstateu.edu/~history/world_history/archives/archive47.html

## Michael D. Meals' Revolutionary War Links Pages
URL: http://www.uconect.net/~histnact/revwar/revwar.html

## Index to History Network Resources
URL: http://blair.library.rhodes.edu/histhtmls/histnet.html#North American

## Horus' Web Links to History Resources
URL: http://www.ucr.edu/h-gig/horuslinks.html

## Utah State Archives Hotlinks!
URL: http://utstdpwww.state.ut.us/~archives/referenc/!history.htm#HistoryR

## Historic Documents of the United States of North America
URL: http://www.ukans.edu/carrie/docs/docs_us.html

## American Civil War: Resources on the Internet
URL: http://www.dsu.edu/%7ejankej/civilwar.html

## The American Revolution: On-Line
URL: http://users.southeast.net/~dixe/amrev/amrev.htm

## Library of Congress: Historical Collections for the National Digital Library
URL: http://rs6.loc.gov/amhome.html

# Ezine

## American History: The Magazine of the American Experience
URL: http://www.thehistorynet.com/AmericanHistory/

# Monstrous Media Kit
**(formerly Kid's Studio)**
The award-winning multimedia creativity tool for kids ages seven to seventeen.

**P**roduce, direct and star in your own multimedia productions. CyberPuppy's Monstrous Media Kit is an all-in-one multimedia application that offers children sophisticated tools for creating their own presentations. Kids can compose brilliant pages combining photo-realistic images with paint, text, and sound, and show off their work as full-screen slide shows, movies or printed stories. Features a "Treasure Chest" of images, Cookie-Cutter Technology, QuickTime™ or Video for Windows, and Kodak PhotoCDs.

**Special pricing for the CD-ROM version:**
• Home or School Edition — for one user $22
• Lab Pack with 5 CDs — for up to five users $65
• Classroom Pack with 5 CDs — for up to 30 users $185
• Network Pack with 5 CDs — for up to 50 users $325
• Site License with 5 CDs — unlimited use in one school building $400

**For more information, contact:**
CyberPuppy Software
2248 Park Boulevard
 Palo ALto, CA  94306
Telephone: (415) 326-2449
Fax: (415) 326-6301
URL: http://www.cyberpuppy.com

**Minimum Requirements, Macintosh:** Mac LC or higher; CD-ROM drive; System 7; 5 MB RAM, 5MB free hard disk space;12-inch monitor with 256 colors/grays.

**Minimum Requirements, Windows:** 486SX; CD-ROM drive; Windows 3.1; 8MB RAM, 5 MB free hard disk space; VGA+ (640 x 480 at 256 colors)

# iCD Educator's INTERNET CD Club

*Classroom-ready Internet™*

**New! Internet on CD-ROM**

## Join the Educator's Internet CD Club today — and receive a year's worth of Internet resources on CD-ROM. No Internet access required!

### iCD — for every subject area and grade level

As an iCD Club member, you'll receive four CDs during the school year. Every iCD is packed full of actual Web sites organized by subject area including: science, mathematics, language arts, world cultures, and more! You'll get great multimedia Web sites appropriate for every subject area and every grade level!

### You have total control!

When you use the Educator's Internet CD Club, you can feel confident that your students will always have access to the sites you've designated. You also don't have to worry about students accessing any "inappropriate material" — because there isn't any — just pure information developed for classroom use.

### Here's what you'll get:

- Actual Internet Web Sites — Six to eight different subject areas chock full of the best Web sites edited and reformatted for classroom use.
- Lesson Plans — Each subject area contains ready-to-use lesson plans.
- Activity Sheets — Gradable activity sheets for each subject area make assessment easy.
- Teaching Tips — Dozens of ideas, "mini-lessons," and added resources to further help you integrate the Educator's Internet CD Club into your classroom.
- Educator's IdeaBank — Lesson plans for any curriculum, classroom software, project ideas and other "teacher-only" resources that will help you enhance all of your educational programs.

### Here's how the iCD Club works:

When you join the Educator's Internet CD Club, you'll receive four CD-ROMs — one iCD will be sent to you every 7–8 weeks during the school year. As a Charter member of the iCD Club, you'll pay the special Charter Member rate of ONLY $129 for the year (a $40 savings off the regular rate).

### Membership

**$129**
Item No. PUB 03
Annual Membership includes 4 CD-ROMs
Plus FREE Teachers Resource PowerPak CD

**Plus**, as an iCD member, you'll also be able to buy **subject-specific CDs** as they become available at the discount membership price of ONLY $19.95 — A 50% savings off the regular price of $39.95. Subjects include math, science, astronomy, social studies and more!

### Netscape 2.0 included!

Each iCD PowerPak comes equipped with 2.0 *(for educational use only)*, the latest in Web browser technology. And we've included six multimedia player programs.

### Special Bonus CD FREE, if you act now!

As a limited time offer, you'll receive absolutely FREE with your membership, the Teacher's Resource PowerPak CD — a $39.95 value! This CD is packed with "teacher only" resources and Internet teaching tips and techniques. Includes actual Internet Web sites for teachers and multimedia software. Includes 30 days FREE Internet access featuring Netscape Navigator™ software

"This is a way to get more kids to use the Net and its wealth of information, even for those who only have one or NO phone lines! It makes the Web portable."

— Barb Falkenburg
Library/Media Specialist
Edgewood, MD

*"You're going to love using iCD in the classroom — brilliant multimedia resources, lesson plans, and project ideas — all classroom-ready for your immediate use."*

## (800) 638-1639

24 hour Fax Line (717) 393-5752
URL: http://www.classroom.net

**TM**

**The way you do research.™**
http://www.k12.elibrary.com/classroom

◆ A complete online research library.

◆ Deep and broad consumer reference product.

◆ The best way for students and families to do research.

◆ Content is as safe as local public library.

◆ Accessible via the Internet.

◆ Updated daily via satellite.

Using The Electric Library, a student can pose a question in plain English and launch a comprehensive and simultaneous search through more than 150 full-text newspapers, over 900 full-text magazines, two international newswires, two thousand classic books, hundreds of maps, thousands of photographs as well as major works of literature and art.

In a matter of seconds, query results are returned to a user ranked in relevancy order, displaying reference data, file size, and grade reading level. With this easy-to-use product a researcher need only click on the document or image of interest and it is automatically downloaded. The materials can also be copied and saved into a word processing document with bibliographic information automatically transferred.

Included in The Electric Library database are materials from world renowned publishers such as Reuters, Simon and Schuster, Gannett, World Almanac, Times Mirror, and Compton's New Media. The Electric Library also incorporates a host of local, ethnic, and special interest publications.

All retrieved information can be downloaded and saved or transferred to a word processor in real time, and used for educational purposes. This includes both the text and images from The Electric Library's databases.

## PARTIAL LIST OF ELECTRIC LIBRARY CONTENT

**Magazines/Journals**
Art Journal
The Economist
Editor & Publisher
Inc.
Lancet
Maclean's
Mother Jones
National Review
New Republic
World Press Review

**Books/Reference Works**
3,000 Great Works of Literature
Monarch Notes
The Complete Works of Shakespeare
The World's Best Poetry
Compton's Encyclopedia
King James Bible
Thematic Dictionary
Webster's Dictionary
World Fact Book

**Newspapers/Newswires**
Baseball Weekly
Jerusalem Post
La Prensa
Los Angeles Times
Magill's Survey of Cinema
Newsbytes News Service
News India
New York Newsday
Reuters
USA Today

**FREE 30-DAY TRIAL!**
Offer made in special arrangement with Classroom Connect

**PRICING**
Individual User: $9.95 per month
School Site License: $2,000 per year

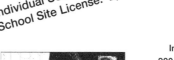

(800) 638-1639

*Infonautics*
**i!**

Infonautics Corporation
900 W. Valley Rd., Suite 1000
Wayne, PA 19087-1830
Voice: (800) 304-3542
Fax: (610) 971-8859
Email: k12@infonautics.com

# *Teaching American History with the Internet* Companion CD-ROM

## *Free software to get you up and running on the Internet right away*

Here is your CD-ROM, jam-packed with free software to get you onto the Internet and using its resources in minutes! There are seven main items on the disc:

1. ***Teaching Language Arts with the Internet HotPage.*** Contains "live" Internet links to many of the best online sites listed throughout this book.

2. ***Internet access software.*** From EarthLink Network,® this includes EarthLink Network TotalAccess™ software with Netscape Navigator.™ The software entitles you to 10 days free, unlimited dial-in Internet access with no sign-up fee.

3. ***SurfWatch™ Internet access management utility.*** Used by parents and teachers to control children's access to the Internet. When SurfWatch is installed on a computer, children have less chance of being accidentally or deliberately exposed to unwanted material. (Included with the Earthlink Network TotalAccess™ software

4. ***HyperStudio™ multimedia software demo.*** Enables you to use the multimedia files you find on the Internet to create colorful, interactive slide shows. This demo version also includes close to 200 MB of clip art, video clips, sounds, and other multimedia files.

5. ***Monstrous Media Kit for Macintosh.*** Multimedia authoring software that is perfect for students who are new to computers and want to create fun, informative interactive presentations with sounds and video.

6. ***CyberPatrol™ Internet access filter software.*** A highly flexible and effective means for blocking access to inappropriate online sites. The version on this CD-ROM is enabled for a full 30-day free trial, after that time you can upgrade to the full version for only $29.00, which includes a one year subscription to the cybernot site blocking list (a $17.95 value—FREE).

7. ***Electric Library™ software.*** Provides an outstanding online research collection. This version is enabled for a full 30-day free trial—a whole month's access to a complete online research library.

**—CD-ROM is Mac/Windows Compatible—**

# Bonus Site Included

*In addition, there is a bonus site on your companion CD-ROM. The site, compliments of Classroom Connect's iCD Club, is:*

**White House Web Site**
URL: http://www2.whitehouse.gov/WH/Welcome.html

The White House site contains information about the current and past presidents. It also offers reference material on the art in the White House, a virtual tour, a Kid's Tour hosted by Socks the cat, and a virtual visit to the President Bill Clinton's office.

## How do I run the CD-ROM on my computer?

This is a hybrid CD-ROM, which means it will work with either an IBM-compatible PC running Windows 3.1/Windows 95 or a Macintosh computer running System 7.5. We recommend that you have at least 8 megabytes of RAM to navigate the Internet and use the included software.

To install, simply load the CD-ROM into your CD drive. Then, using any word-processing program, look for a file called READ ME (on the Mac) or README.TXT (on a PC). The file contains complete instructions on how to load the CD-ROM.

# Notes

# Notes

# Notes

# Notes

# Notes

# Notes

# Notes